Who Likes Rain?

Wong Herbert Yee

Wright Group

The **McGraw·Hill** Companies

For Christy

www.WrightGroup.com

 **Wright Group**

Send all inquiries to:
Wright Group/McGraw-Hill
P.O. Box 812960
Chicago, IL 60681

ISBN 978-0-07-658166-5
MHID 0-07-658166-7

2 3 4 5 6 7 8 9 DRN 16 15 14 13 12 11 10

Pit-pit-pit on the windowpane.

Down, down, down come the drops of rain.

Who wants rain?

Who needs April showers?

I know who…

The trees and the flowers!

Raindrops falling
Down in spring
Hit the awning,
Ping-ping-ping!

When it rains,

Who's the first to scat?

I know! Do you?

Mew, mew...

It's the cat!

Gurgle, gurgle
Down the gutters
Out the spout
The water splutters.

Who likes rain?

Not Papa's old truck.

Who likes rain?

Quack, quack…

It's a duck!

Pitty-plip-PLOP,
Pitty-pat-SPLAT!
I can catch raindrops,
In my hat.

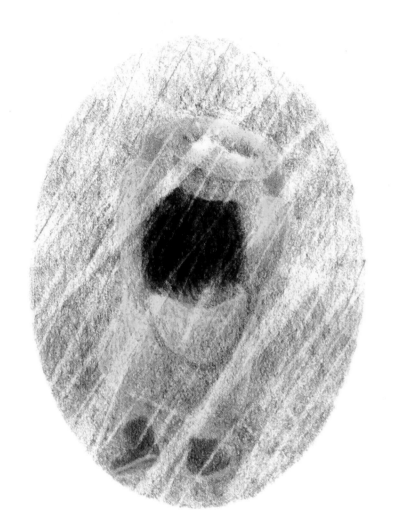

When it rains,

Who comes out to squirm?

I know! Do you?

Creep, creep...

It's a worm!

Raindrops beat like a tom-tom drum

On my umbrella, *rum-a-tum-tum!*

Who likes rain?

Not my neighbor's dog.

Who likes rain?

Croak, croak...

It's a frog!

A wind comes *whooshing*
Through the trees.
It shakes the raindrops
From the leaves.

Who likes rain?

It jumps with a *splish!*

I know! Do you?

Glub, glub...

It's a fish!

After a while the showers stop.

A few last drops fall, *plip-plip—PLOP!*

Clouds break up, no need to huddle.

All that's left is ...

...one BIG puddle.

Who likes rain even more than a duck?

More than a frog in the muckety-muck?

Who needs rain besides trees and flowers?

Who wants a day with April showers?

Off comes the raincoat,

boots, and hat.

Who likes rain?

I do!

KER-*SPLAT!*